A CATALOGUE OF COMIC VERSE

Collected and
illustrated by

Rolf Harris

From an original compilation by
Patricia Nicholson

KNIGHT BOOKS
Hodder and Stoughton

British Library C.I.P.

A Catalogue of comic verse.
1. Humorous poetry, English
I. Harris, Rolf II. Nicholson Patricia
821'.07'08   PR1195.H8

ISBN 0-340-42387-0

Printed and bound in Great Britain for Hodder and Stoughton Paperbacks, a division of Hodder and Stoughton Ltd., Mill Road, Dunton Green, Sevenoaks, Kent TN13 2YA (Editorial Office: 47 Bedford Square, London WC1B 3DP) by Clays Ltd., St Ives plc

CONTENTS

INTRODUCTION

For me, comic poems are a lot like cartoons. If they're going to work, they must have a good, unexpected, funny idea before anything else happens.

Once you've got that basic idea, the next step, if it's a poem, is to dress it up and refine it, or in some cases, prune it down and simplify it, in the best way you can, and hopefully leave the comedy twist until the last possible moment.

It's like a good joke, isn't it?

My approach with the cartoons was either to see if I could add even further to the comedy by putting in outrageous things that first occurred to me when I read that particular poem, or, to try and draw an exact representation of the really outlandish funny thoughts that were already there. I hope you think the drawings help. (I've managed to get quite a few of my favourite cats into the picture . . . Well, it IS a CAT-alogue you know!)

There's a lot of space where you can do your *own* drawings if you want to – you could even write a few silly poems yourself – as Shel Silverstein says in his poem PUT SOMETHING IN:

> Write a nutty poem,
> Sing a mumble-gumble song,
> Whistle through your comb.

Do a loony-goony dance
'Cross the kitchen floor,
Put something silly in the world
That ain't been there before.

Do it! You could have as much fun as we've all
had.

MOSTLY ME...

MY NOSE

It doesn't breathe;
It doesn't smell;
It doesn't feel
So very well.

I am discouraged
With my nose:
The only thing it
Does is blows.

Dorothy Aldis

ELBOWS

The elbow has a certain charm
By being halfway up your arm.
Without it you'd be less than able
But never leave it on the table.

Max Fatchen

5

LATE FOR BREAKFAST

Who is it hides my sandals when I'm trying
   to get dressed?
And takes away the hairbrush that was lying
   on the chest?
I want to start breakfast before any of the
   others
But something's always missing or been
   borrowed by my brothers.
I think I'd better dress at night, and eat my
   breakfast too,
      Then when everybody's hurrying –
      I'll have nothing else to do.

                                    Mary Dawson

PLEASE EXPLAIN

Have you ever tried explaining
A sundial to a bat,
Or taught a muddy little brother
The usage of a mat?
Have you ever tried explaining
A desert to a fish,
Or found a single wishing-well
In which you didn't want to wish?
If you have succeeded
Then please explain to me
Why it's always sunny at school-time
And rainy after tea.

                                    Brian Patten

FROM: A CHRISTMAS PACKAGE

My stocking's where
He'll see it – there!
One-half a pair.

The tree is sprayed,
My prayers are prayed,
My wants are weighed.

I've made a list
Of what he missed
Last year. I've kissed

My father, mother,
Sister, brother;
I've done those other

Things I should
And would and could.
So far, so good.

David McCord

FOUR SEASONS

Spring is showery, flowery, bowery.
Summer: hoppy, choppy, poppy.
Autumn: wheezy, sneezy, freezy.
Winter: slippy, drippy, nippy.

anon

THE FROGOLOGIST

I hate it when grown-ups say,
'What do you want to be?'
I hate the way they stand up there
And talk down to me.

I say:

'I want to be a frogologist
And study the lives of frogs,
I want to know their habitat
And crawl about in bogs,
I want to learn to croak and jump
And catch flies with my tongue
And will they please excuse me 'cause
Frogologists start quite young.'

Brian Patten

Do you prefer
giblets or triplets,
or triplets to giblets,
or not?
Do you like carrots
as dearly as parrots,
or parrots far better,
or what?

Do you prefer
lizards to blizzards,
and blizzards and lizards
to lumps?
Do you like wrinkles
better than crinkles
and crinkles much better
than mumps?

Do you think slippers
are better than flippers,
and flippers are better
than flaps?
Then don't ever bother
to marry another.
We were meant for each other!
Perhaps.

N. M. Bodecker

THE MUDDY PUDDLE

I am sitting
In the middle
Of a rather Muddy
Puddle,
With my bottom
Full of bubbles
And my rubbers
Full of Mud,

While my jacket
And my sweater
Go on slowly
Getting wetter
As I very
Slowly settle
To the Bottom
Of the Mud.

And I find that
What a person
With a puddle
Round his middle
Thinks of mostly
In the muddle
Is the Muddi-
Ness of Mud.

Dennis Lee

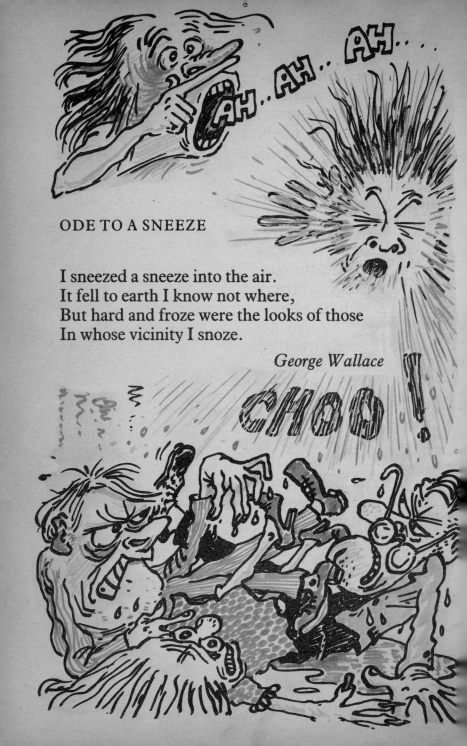

ODE TO A SNEEZE

I sneezed a sneeze into the air.
It fell to earth I know not where,
But hard and froze were the looks of those
In whose vicinity I snooze.

George Wallace

JUNE

June's come – blue skies,
The air full of butterflies;
They perch on the flowers.
We watch them for hours.

'I want to fly like that!'
'So do I.' 'So do I.'
'Well, we can try.'

We make ourselves wings
Out of paper and things.
Paint them all brightly,
Tie them with strings.

'Mine is a Swallowtail!'
'Mine's a Red Admiral!'
'Mine is a Meadow Brown!'
'Mine is a Chalk Hill Blue!'
'Mine's an invented kind!'
Yes, that is true.

We jump up and down,
We leap and we bound,
But always come back
To the ground.
Now why is that?
Perhaps we are too fat.

But our wings had their flight.
Each pair made a kite.
They flew – such a height!
So *that* was all right.

Naomi Lewis

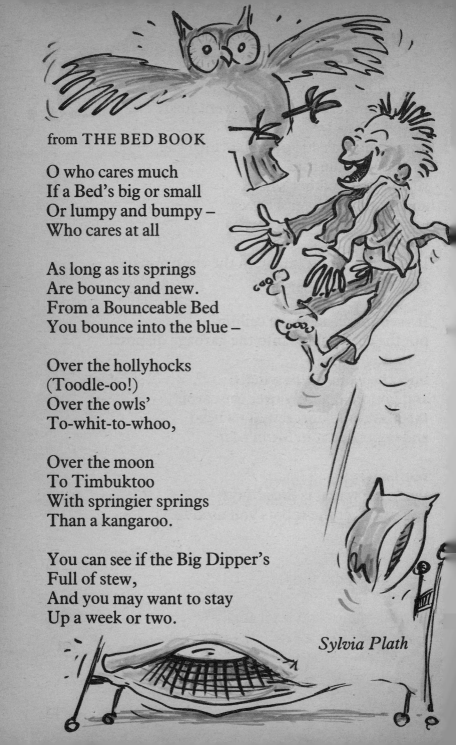

from THE BED BOOK

O who cares much
If a Bed's big or small
Or lumpy and bumpy –
Who cares at all

As long as its springs
Are bouncy and new.
From a Bounceable Bed
You bounce into the blue –

Over the hollyhocks
(Toodle-oo!)
Over the owls'
To-whit-to-whoo,

Over the moon
To Timbuktoo
With springier springs
Than a kangaroo.

You can see if the Big Dipper's
Full of stew,
And you may want to stay
Up a week or two.

Sylvia Plath

DOMESTIC HELP

The other day,
one of our domestic robots went mad,
kissed my dad,
poured marmalade over the videowall,
shampooed the cat,
sugared my mother's hair,
and sat on my sister's knee
(she fell through the chair).

Dad's frantic fiddling with the control-panel
only made matters worse.

It vacuum-cleaned the ceiling,
put the coffee-table into the garbage disposal
    unit,
uncorked a bottle of wine
and poured it gently over the carpet,
then carefully unscrewed its head
and deposited it in Mum's lap.

Mother says
that's the way it is these days:
you can't get the robots you used to.

Adrian Henri

'Let's see some super shapes you Blue
    Group,'
Mr Lavender shouts down the hall.
'And forests don't forget your trembly leaves
And stand up straight and tall.'

But Phillip Chubb is in our group
And he wants to be Robin Hood
And Ann Boot is sulking because she's not
    with her friend
And I don't see why I should be wood.

The lights are switched on in the class-
    rooms,
Outside the sky's nearly black.
And the dining-hall smells of gravy and fat
And Chubb has boils down his back.

Sir tells him straight that he's got to be tree
But he won't wave his arms around.
'How can I wave my branches, Sir,
Friar Tuck has chopped them all down.'

Then I come cantering through Sherwood
To set Maid Marion free
And I really believe I'm Robin Hood
And the Sheriff's my enemy.

At my back my trusty longbow
My broadsword clanks at my side,
My outlaws gallop behind me
As into adventure we ride.

'Untie that maid you villain,' I shout
With all the strength I have,
But the tree has got bored and is picking his
    nose
And Maid Marion has gone to the lav.

After rehearsals, Sir calls us together
And each group performs their play,
But just as it comes to our turn
The bell goes for the end of the day.

As I trudge my way home through the city
    streets
The cars and the houses retreat
And a thunder of hooves beats in my mind
And I gallop through acres of wheat.

The castle gleams white in the distance,
The banners flap, golden and red,
And distant trumpets weave silver dreams
In the landscapes of my head.

                                        Gareth Owen

SAY PLEASE

I'll have a please sandwich cheese
No I mean a knees sandwich please
Sorry I mean a fleas sandwich please
No a please sandwich please
no   no –
I'll have a doughnut

                                        Michael Rosen

Nothing can really beat
For a quick sensuous treat
Clean socks on just-bathed feet.

How does your little toe
In the bed so long and bare
Keep on discovering
The top sheet's little tear?

Roy Fuller

THE PLUG-HOLE MAN

I know you're down there, Plug-hole Man,
    In the dark so utter,
For when I let the water out
    I hear you gasp and splutter.

And though I peer and peek and pry
    I've never seen you yet:
(I know you're down there, Plug-hole Man,
    In your home so wet).

But you will not be there for long
    For I've a *plan*, you see;
I'm going to catch you, Plug-hole Man,
    And Christian's helping me.

We'll fill the bath with water hot,
    Then give the plug a heave,
And rush down to the outside drain –
    And *catch* you as you leave!

Carey Blyton

I'M A GROWN MAN NOW

I'm a grown man now
Don't easily scare
(if you don't believe me
ask my teddy bear).

Roger McGough

THE FLOATING FLAUTIST

I wish I lived in a house in the clouds:
I'd serenade wing-clapping seagull crowds.
My flute would purr and ripple and trill
And angels would perch on my window-sill.

Adrian Mitchell

MY SISTER LAURA

My sister Laura's bigger than me
And lifts me up quite easily.
I can't lift her, I've tried and tried;
She must have something heavy inside.

Spike Milligan

GOING THROUGH THE OLD PHOTOS

Who's that?
That's your Auntie Mabel
and that's me
under the table.

Who's that?
That's Uncle Billy.
Who's that?
Me being silly.

Who's that
licking a lolly?
I'm not sure
but I think it's Polly.

Who's that
behind the tree?
I don't know
I can't see.
Could be you.
Could be me.

Who's that?
Baby Joe.
Who's that?
I don't know.

Who's that standing
on his head?
Turn it round.
It's Uncle Ted.

Michael Rosen

SISTER

Tell me a story!
Lend me that book!
Please, let me come in your den?
I won't mess it up,
so *please* say I can.
When? When? When?

Lend me that engine,
that truck – and your glue.
I'll give you half of my old bubblegum.
You know what Dad said
about learning to share.
Give it *now* –
or I'm telling Mum!

Oh, *please* lend your bike –
I'll be careful this time.
I'll keep out of the mud
and the snow.
I could borrow your hat –
the one you've just got . . .

said my sister

And I said

NO!

Judith Nicholls

27

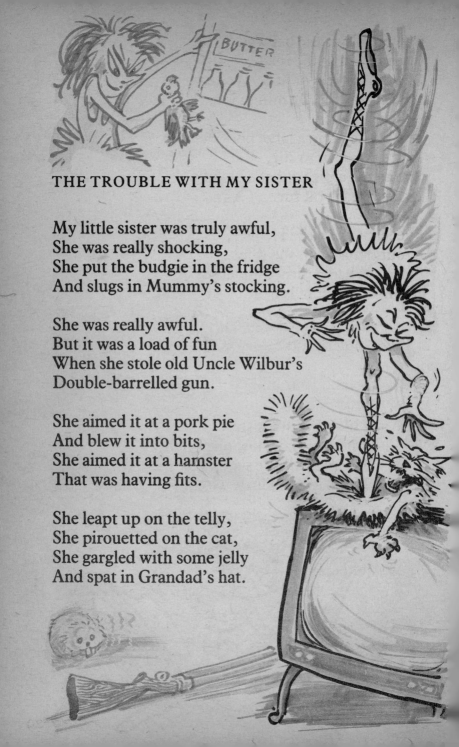

THE TROUBLE WITH MY SISTER

My little sister was truly awful,
She was really shocking,
She put the budgie in the fridge
And slugs in Mummy's stocking.

She was really awful.
But it was a load of fun
When she stole old Uncle Wilbur's
Double-barrelled gun.

She aimed it at a pork pie
And blew it into bits,
She aimed it at a hamster
That was having fits.

She leapt up on the telly,
She pirouetted on the cat,
She gargled with some jelly
And spat in Grandad's hat.

She ran down the hallway,
She ran across the road,
She dug up lots of little worms
And caught a squirming toad.

She put them in a large pot
And she began to stir,
She added a pint of bat's blood
And some rabbit fur.

She leapt upon the Hoover,
Around the room she went.
Once she had a turned-up nose
But now her nose is bent.

I like my little sister,
There is really just one hitch,
I think my little sister
Has become a little witch.   *Brian Patten*

James James
Morrison Morrison
Weatherby George Dupree
Took great
Care of his Mother,
Though he was only three.
James James
Said to his Mother,
'Mother,' he said, said he;
'You must never go down to the end of the
    town, if you don't go down with me.'
James James
Morrison's Mother
Put on a golden gown,
James James
Morrison's Mother
Drove to the end of the town.
James James
Morrison's Mother
Said to herself, said she:
'I can get right down to the end of the town
    and be back in time for tea.'

King John
Put up a notice,
'LOST or STOLEN or STRAYED!
JAMES JAMES
MORRISON'S MOTHER
SEEMS TO HAVE BEEN MISLAID.
LAST SEEN
WANDERING VAGUELY:

QUITE OF HER OWN ACCORD,
SHE TRIED TO GET DOWN TO THE END OF
THE TOWN – FORTY SHILLINGS REWARD!'

James James
Morrison Morrison
(Commonly known as Jim)
Told his
Other relations
Not to go blaming *him*.
James James
Said to his Mother,
'Mother,' he said, said he:
'You must *never* go down to the end of the
  town without consulting me.'

James James
Morrison's mother
Hasn't been heard of since.
King John
Said he was sorry,
So did the Queen and Prince.
King John
(Somebody told me)
Said to a man he knew:
'If people go down to the end of the town,
  well, what can *anyone do*?'

(*Now then, very softly*)
  J. J.
  M. M.
  W. G. Du P.
  Took great
  C/o his M*****

Though he was only 3.
J. J.
Said to his M*****
'M*****,' he said, said he:

'You-must-never-go-down-to-the-end-of-
  the-town-if-you-don't-go-down-with-ME!'

A. A. Milne

COUSIN REGGIE

Cousin Reggie
who adores the sea
lives in the Midlands
unfortunately.

He surfs down escalators
in department stores
and swims the High Street
on all of his fours.

Sunbathes on the pavement
paddles in the gutter
(I think our Reggie's
a bit of a nutter).

Roger McGough

MY OTHER GRANNY

My Granny is an Octopus
    At the bottom of the sea,
And when she comes to supper
    She brings her family.

She chooses a wild wet windy night
    When the world rolls blind
As a boulder in the night-sea surf,
    And her family troops behind.

The sea-smell enters with them
    As they sidle and slither and spill
With their huge eyes and their tiny eyes
    And a dripping ocean-chill.

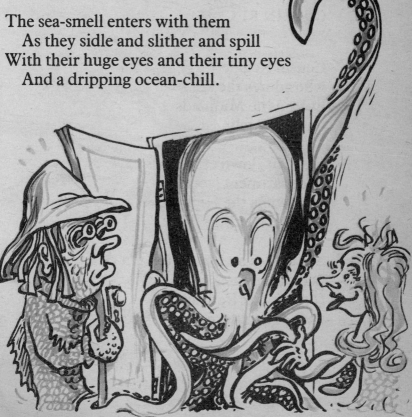

Some of her cousins are lobsters
    Some floppy jelly fish –
What would you be if your family tree
    Grew out of such a dish?

Her brothers are crabs jointed and knobbed
    With little pinhead eyes,
Their pincers crack the biscuits
    And they bubble joyful cries.

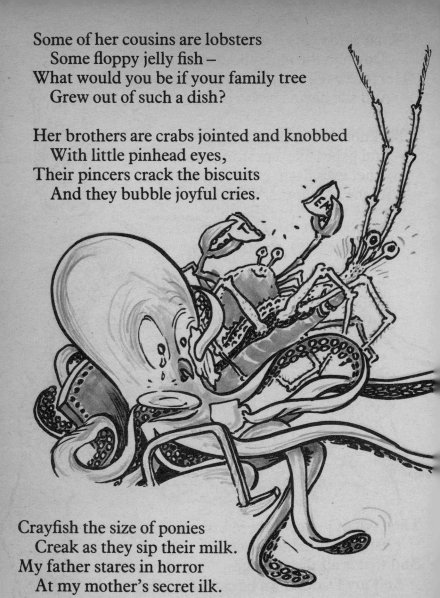

Crayfish the size of ponies
    Creak as they sip their milk.
My father stares in horror
    At my mother's secret ilk.

They wave long whiplash antennae,
    They sizzle and they squirt –
We smile and waggle our fingers back
    Or grandma would be hurt.

'What's new, Ma?' my father asks,
　'Down in the marvellous deep?'
Her face swells up, her eyes bulge huge
　And she begins to weep.

She knots her sucker tentacles
　And gapes like a nestling bird,
And her eyes flash, changing stations,
　As she attempts a WORD –

Then out of her eyes there brim two drops
　That plop into her saucer –
And that is all she manages,
　And my Dad knows he can't force her.

And when they've gone, my ocean-folk,
　No man could prove they came –
For the sea-tears in her saucer
　And a man's tears are the same.

Ted Hughes

I'd sooner be
Jumped and thumped and dumped

I'd sooner be
Slugged and mugged . . . than *hugged* . . .

And clobbered with a slobbering
Kiss by Auntie Jean:

You know what I mean;

Whenever she comes to stay,
You know you're bound

To get one.
A quick
   short
   peck
   would
   be
   O.K.
But this is a
Whacking great
Smacking great
Wet one!

All whoosh and spit
And crunch and squeeze
And '*Dear* little boy!'
And 'Auntie's missed you!'

And 'Come to Auntie, she
Hasn't *kissed* you!'
Please don't do it, Auntie,
PLEASE!

Or if you've absolutely
Got to,

And nothing on *earth* can persuade you
Not to,

The trick
Is to make it
Quick,

You know what I mean?

For as things are,
I really would far,

Far sooner be
Jumped and thumped and dumped,

I'd sooner be
Slugged and mugged . . . than *hugged* . . .

And clobbered with a slobbering
Kiss by my Auntie

Jean!

                              Kit Wright

MY UNCLE ROBERT

My Uncle Robert
is bald as a coot,
and he polishes his skull
just like a boot.
On a hot day his head
reflects the sun's heat,
burning the soles
of flying birds' feet.

Michael Dugan

THE SOCIAL MIXER

Father said, 'Heh heh! I'll fix her!' –
Threw mother in the concrete mixer.

She whirled about and called, 'Come hither!'
It looked like fun. He jumped in with her.

Then in to join that dizzy dance
Jumped Auntie Bea and Uncle Anse.

In leaped my little sister Lena
And Chuckling Chuck her pet hyena.

Even Granmaw Fanshaw felt a yearning
To do some high-speed overturning.

All shouted through the motor's whine
'Aw, come on in – the concrete's fine!'

I jumped in too and got all scrambly.
What a crazy mixed-up family.

X. J. Kennedy

When grandma visits you, my dears,
    Be as good as you can be;
Don't put hot waffles in her ears,
    Or beetles in her tea.

Don't sew a pattern on her cheek
    With worsted or with silk;
Don't call her naughty names in Greek,
    Or spray her face with milk.

Don't drive a staple in her foot,
    Don't stick pins in her head;
And, oh, I beg you, do not put
    Live embers in her bed.

These things are not considered kind;
    They worry her, and tease –
Such cruelty is not refined
    It always fails to please.

Be good to grandma, little chaps,
    Whatever else you do;
And then she'll grow to be – perhaps –
    More tolerant of you.

anon

BABBLING AND GABBLING

My Granny's an absolute corker,
My Granny's an absolute cracker,
But she's Britain's speediest talker
And champion yackety-yacker!

Everyone's fond of my Granny,
Everyone thinks she's nice,
But before you can say Jack Robinson,
My Granny's said it twice!

Kit Wright

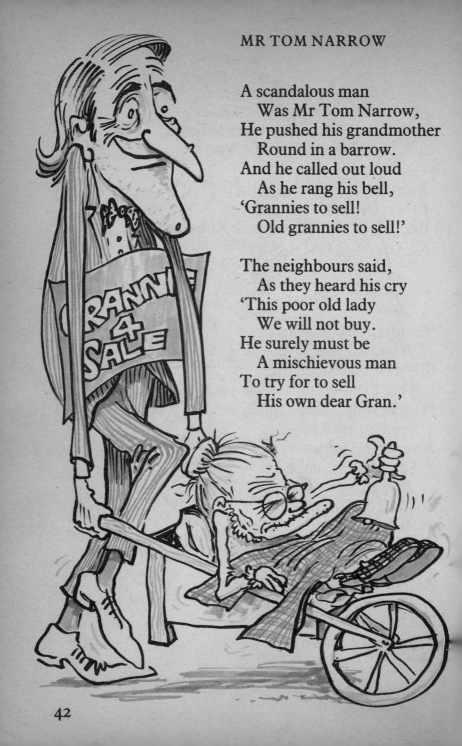

MR TOM NARROW

A scandalous man
    Was Mr Tom Narrow,
He pushed his grandmother
    Round in a barrow.
And he called out loud
    As he rang his bell,
'Grannies to sell!
    Old grannies to sell!'

The neighbours said,
    As they heard his cry
'This poor old lady
    We will not buy.
He surely must be
    A mischievous man
To try for to sell
    His own dear Gran.'

GRANNIES
4
SALE

'Besides,' said another,
   'If you ask me,
She'd be very small use
   That I can see.'
'You're right,' said a third,
   'And no mistake –
A very poor bargain
   She'd surely make.'

So Mr Tom Narrow
   He scratched his head,
And he sent his grandmother
   Back to bed;
And he rang his bell
   Through all the town
Till he sold his barrow
   For half a crown.

James Reeves

43

FOR YEARS

For years you've greeted me with frowns
I thought it just your style.
I can't forget, the day I met
The horror of your smile!

Pixie O'Harris

WELCOME!

WHISKERS ALONE ARE BAD ENOUGH

'Whiskers alone are bad enough
Attached to faces coarse and rough;
But how much greater their offence is
When stuck on Uncles' countenances.'

Norman Lindsay

THE CABBAGE IS A FUNNY VEG.

The cabbage is a funny veg.
All crisp, and green, and brainy
I sometimes wear one on my head
When it's cold and rainy.

Roger McGough

49

GREEN WATERCRESS

Now there's nothing about which I really
    knew less
Than the care and the culture of green
    watercress.
But I searched and I searched and I finally
    found
That it grew in the water and not in the
    ground.
So I planted some seeds and the very next
    day
I found that the water had washed them
    away.
So I bought me some sinkers and bought me
    some twine,
And I anchored them down and they're now
    doing fine.

Rolf Harris

SLIP WARE

There's many a slip
Twix cup and lip,
And the sound it makes
Is drip drip drip.

Spike Milligan

GIANTS' DELIGHT

Vats of soup
On table trays
Side of shark
With mayonnaise
Haunch of ox
With piles of mice
Mounds of gristle
Served on ice
Bone of mammoth
Head of boar
Whales and serpents
By the score
Tons of cole slaw
Stacks of rabbits
(Giants have such
Piggy habits)
Then, at last,
There comes a stew
Full of buffalo
And ewe
Followed by
Some chocolate cakes
Big enough
For stomachaches

Steven Kroll

CELERY

Celery, raw,
Develops the jaw,
But celery, stewed,
Is more quietly chewed.

Ogden Nash

I LIKED GROWING

I liked growing.
That was nice.
The leaves were soft
The sun was hot.
I was warm and red and round
Then someone dropped me in a pot.

Being a strawberry isn't all pleasing.
This morning they put me in ice cream.
I'm freezing.

Karla Kuskin

EAT AWAY, CHEW AWAY

'Eat away, chew away, munch away and bolt
    and guzzle
Never leave the table till you're full up to the
    muzzle.'

Norman Lindsay

THROUGH THE TEETH

Through the teeth
And past the gums.
Look out, stomach,
Here it comes!

anon

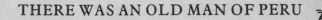

THERE WAS AN OLD MAN OF PERU

There was an old man of Peru,
Who dreamt he was eating his shoe.
   He woke in the night
   In a terrible fright,
And found it was perfectly true.

anon

Oh, who would be a puddin',
  A puddin' in a pot,
A puddin' which is stood on
  A fire which is hot?
O sad indeed the lot
Of puddin's in a pot.

I wouldn't be a puddin'
  If I could be a bird,
If I could be a wooden
  Doll, I would'n say a word.
Yes, I have often heard
It's grand to be a bird.

But as I am a puddin',
  A puddin' in a pot,
I hope you get the stomachache
  For eatin' me a lot.
I hope you get it hot,
You puddin'-eatin' lot!

Norman Lindsay

THERE WAS A YOUNG LAD OF ST JUST

There was a young lad of St Just
Who ate apple pie till he bust.
   It wasn't the fru-it
   That caused him to do it,
What finished him off was the crust.

anon

A REALLY HOT MEAL

A really hot meal
Doesn't appeal
To a Seal.
Its favourite dish
Is very cold fish!

     Gavin Ewart

I sat in the café and sipped at a Coke.
There sat down beside me a WHOPPING great
   bloke
Who sighed as he elbowed me into the wall:
'Your trouble, my boy, is your belly's too
   small!
Your bottom's too thin! Take a lesson from
   me:
I may not be nice, but I'm GREAT, you'll
   agree,
And I've lasted a lifetime by playing this
   hunch:
The bigger the breakfast, the larger the lunch!

The larger the lunch, then the huger the
   supper.
The deeper the teapot, the vaster the cupper.
The fatter the sausage, the fuller the tea.
The MORE on the table, the BETTER for ME!'

His elbows moved in and his elbows moved
   out,
His belly grew bigger, chins wobbled about,
As forkful by forkful and plate after plate,
He ate and he ate and he ate and he ATE!

I hardly could breathe, I was squashed out of
   shape,
So under the table I made my escape.

'Aha!' he rejoiced, 'when it's put to the test,
The fellow who's fattest will come off the
 best!
Remember, my boy, when it comes to the
 crunch:
The bigger the breakfast, the larger the lunch!

The larger the lunch, then the huger the
 supper.
The deeper the teapot, the vaster the cupper.
The fatter the sausage, the fuller the tea.
The MORE on the table, the BETTER for ME!'

A lady came by who was scrubbing the floor
With a mop and a bucket. To even the score,
I lifted that bucket of water and said,
As I poured the whole lot of it over his head:

'*I've* found all my life, it's a pretty sure bet:
The FULLER the bucket, the WETTER you
 GET!'

Kit Wright

HASTEN JASON

HASTEN JASON
FETCH THE BASIN

too late . . . fetch the mop.

anon

LONGING

I wish I was a little grub
With whiskers round my tummy.
I'd climb into a honey-pot
And make my tummy gummy.

anon

BREAKFAST

Is it coffee for breakfast?
I wish it was tea!
Is it jam? Oh, why can't there
Be honey for me?

Is it brown bread-and-butter?
I wish it was toast!
Is it just bread-and-milk?
I like porridge the most.

Is it soft-boiled eggs? Bother!
I'd rather have fried.
You *know* I don't like soft-boiled eggs,
Though I've tried.

Of all horrid breakfasts
This breakfast's the worst! —
Who tumbled out of his bed
Wrong leg first?

Eleanor Farjeon

To Liza and Rick

I EAT MY PEAS WITH HONEY

I eat my peas with honey,
   I've done it all my life:
It makes the peas taste funny,
   But it keeps them on the knife.

anon

i

We can recommend our soups
And offer thick or thin.
One is known as *Packet*,
The other known as *Tin*.

ii

The flying-fish makes a very fine dish;
As good as plaice or skate
When sizzled in fat; but be certain that
You tether it to your plate.

iii

Now this hot-dog makes an excellent snack;
Our sausages are best pork.
If you can't get it down, please don't send it
   back,
But take it for a nice brisk walk.

iv

Are you tempted by our fried fish-fingers?
The last customer to succumb
Was hard to please; he demanded
Why we couldn't provide a fish thumb.

v

Bubble-and-squeak is splendid stuff
And Chef takes endless trouble
But if you feel you'd like a change
Then try our squeak-and-bubble.

Try our cabinet pudding
Or a slice of home-made cake;
We serve with each, quite free of charge,
A pill for your tummy-ache.

Vernon Scannell

NEVER TRY TO MAKE YOUR MEALS

Never try to make your meals
From the big Electric Eels!
Slim, athletic, not fat-bellied,
Never try to serve them jellied!
You would be a laughing-stock –
And you'd get a frightful shock!

Gavin Ewart

AMELIA

Amelia mixed the mustard,
    She mixed it good and thick;
She put it in the custard
    And made her Mother sick,
And showing satisfaction
    By many a loud hurrah,
'Observe,' she said, 'the action
    Of mustard on Mamma.'

A. E. Housman

The orange squiggles lie
Lifeless on your plate,
As though
A modern artist
Has tried to make a
Masterpiece of
Your lunch.

Most people say:
'It looks like worms'
But in
My opinion
That's impossible,
They're too messy, too scraggly
To be worms.

This is where the
Trouble starts,
Here comes the FORK!
The pieces of orange silky wool
Wrap themselves around the
Stainless steel trident.
The spaghetti is moving in
To strangle the helpless fork
Why can't this tangle keep still?
Just behave yourself
Like a sensible meal.

Mark Whittington (13)

I RAISED A GREAT HULLABALOO

I raised a great hullabaloo
When I found a large mouse in my stew,
   Said the waiter, 'Don't shout
   And wave it about,
Or the rest will be wanting one, too!'

anon

THE OLD LADY OF RYE

There was an old lady of Rye
Who was baked by mistake in a pie,
   To the household's disgust
   She emerged through the crust,
And exclaimed, with a yawn, 'Where am I?'

anon

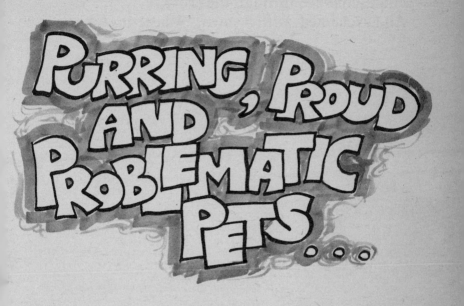

PURRING, PROUD AND PROBLEMATIC PETS...

THE TIGER

A tiger going for a stroll
Met an old man and ate him whole.

The old man shouted, and he thumped.
The tiger's stomach churned and bumped.

The other tigers said: 'Now really,
We hear your breakfast much too clearly.'

The moral is, he should have chewed.
It does no good to bolt one's food.

Edward Lucie-Smith

THERE ONCE WAS A MAN OF BENGAL

There once was a man of Bengal
Who was asked to a fancy dress ball;
He murmured: 'I'll risk it
and go as a biscuit . . .'
But a dog ate him up in the hall.

anon

A MOUSE IN THE KITCHEN

There's a mouse in the kitchen
    Playing skittles with the peas.
He's drinking mugs of coffee
    And eating last week's cheese.

There's a mouse in the kitchen
    We could catch him in a hat.
Otherwise he'll toast the teacakes
    And that's bound to annoy the cat.

There's a mouse in the kitchen
    Ignoring all our wishes.
He's eaten tomorrow's dinner
    But at least he's washed the dishes.

Note
Yes. I'm the mouse in the kitchen
    Thank you for the grub.
I feel quite full but thirsty now
    So I'm nipping down the pub.

John Rice

PEREGRINE

A peregrine named Peregrine
Has never grinned a grin
Because no other peregrine
Has grinned at Peregrine.

Colin West

First he sat, and then he lay,
And then he said: I've come to stay.
And that is how we acquired our doggy
    Pontz.
He is all right as dogs go, but not quite what
    one wants.
Because he talks. He talks like you and me.
And he is not you and me, he is made
    differently.
You think it is nice to have a talking animal?
It is not nice. It is unnatural.

Stevie Smith

HUNTER TRIALS

It's awf'lly bad luck on Diana,
    Her ponies have swallowed their bits;
She fished down their throats with a spanner
    And frightened them all into fits.

So now she's attempting to borrow.
    Do lend her some bits, Mummy, *do*;
I'll lend her my own for tomorrow,
    But today *I*'ll be wanting them too.

Just look at Prunella on Guzzle,
    The wizardest pony on earth;
Why doesn't she slacken his muzzle
    And tighten the breech in his girth?

I say, Mummy, there's Mrs Geyser
    And doesn't she look pretty sick?
I bet it's because Mona Lisa
    Was hit on the hock with a brick.

Miss Blewitt says Monica threw it,
    But Monica says it was Joan,
And Joan's very thick with Miss Blewitt,
    So Monica's sulking alone.

And Margaret failed in her paces,
    Her withers got tied in a noose,
So her coronets caught in the traces
    And now all her fetlocks are loose.

Oh, it's me now. I'm terribly nervous.
    I wonder if Smudges will shy.
She's practically certain to swerve as
    Her Pelham is over one eye.

★   ★   ★

Oh wasn't it naughty of Smudges?
    Oh, Mummy, I'm sick with disgust.
She threw me in front of the Judges,
    And my silly old collarbone's bust.

John Betjeman

I'VE GOT A DOG AS THIN AS A RAIL

I've got a dog as thin as a rail,
He's got fleas all over his tail;
Every time his tail goes flop,
The fleas on the bottom all hop to the top.

anon

THERE WAS A SMALL MAIDEN NAMED MAGGIE

There was a small maiden named Maggie,
Whose dog was enormous and shaggy;
The front end of him
Looked vicious and grim –
But the tail end was friendly and waggy.

anon

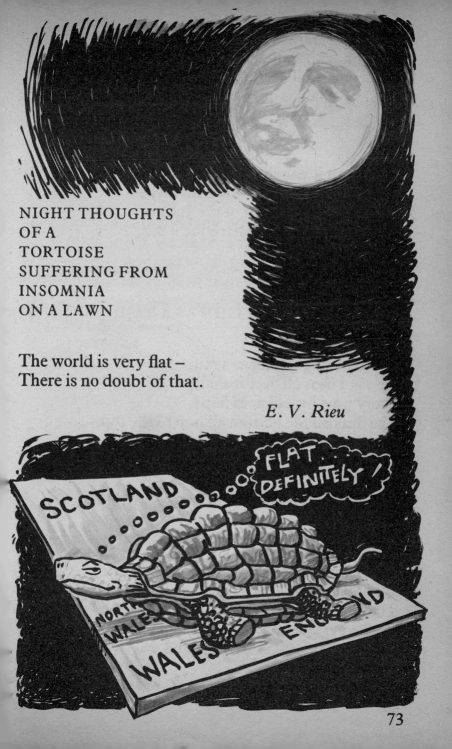

NIGHT THOUGHTS
OF A
TORTOISE
SUFFERING FROM
INSOMNIA
ON A LAWN

The world is very flat –
There is no doubt of that.

E. V. Rieu

AUNTIE BABS

Auntie Babs became besotted
With her snake, so nicely spotted,
Unaware that pets so mottled
Like to leave their keepers throttled.

Colin West

MY UNCLE PAUL OF PIMLICO

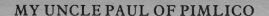

My Uncle Paul of Pimlico
Has seven cats as white as snow,
Who sit at his enormous feet
And watch him, as a special treat,
Play the piano upside down,
In his delightful dressing-gown;
The firelight leaps, the parlour glows,
And, while the music ebbs and flows,
They smile (while purring the refrains),
At little thoughts that cross their brains.

Mervyn Peake

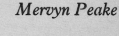

SOMETHING SILLY

THE FASTEST TRAIN IN THE WORLD

Tokyo to Kyoto
   tokyotokyoto
kyotokyotokyotokyo
   tokyotokyoto

Keith Bosley

THE CATERPILLAR

For some people pets
   Have to miaow and to purr,
Have to swish long tails
   And have warm fur.

For others the pets
   Must be fished from a lake:
Must have glittering scales
   And fishfood to take.

Still others like those
   That scurry and bark.
That chew socks and dig
   Shallow holes in the dark.

But the strangest companion
   That I ever knew
Was a smart tartan caterpillar
   Who lived in a shoe.

He had hair on his back
   And dozens of feet
But refused to be brushed
   Or to walk down the street.

He was long and quite slender,
   He could bend like a spring,
And he looked like a colourful
   Piece of old string.

He liked leaves and was fussy
   About their condition:
If he didn't approve
   He'd reverse his position.

He was quaint, though, and curious—
   A rather strange friend—
But like all really good things
   He came to an end.

He took to the air
   One wonderful day
And waved (or I think so)
   As he fluttered away.

And now when I'm walking
   And see red, yellow, blue.
I think of the winged one
   Who came from a shoe.

Alan Bold

ONE FINE DAY IN THE MIDDLE OF THE NIGHT

One fine day in the middle of the night
Two dead men got up to fight,
Two blind men to see fair play,
Two dumb men to shout 'Hurray!'
And two lame men to carry them away.

anon

THE RABBIT'S CHRISTMAS CAROL

I'm sick as a parrot,
I've lost me carrot,
I couldn't care less if it's
Christmas Day.

I'm sick as a parrot,
I've lost me carrot,
So get us a lettuce
Or . . . go away!

Kit Wright

A SONG OF THANKS

It's sensible that icicles
    Hang downward as they grow,
For I would hate to step on one
    That's buried in the snow.

It's really best that tides come in
    And then return to sea;
For if they kept on coming in,
    How wet we all would be!

I've often thought tomatoes are
    Much better red than blue,
A blue tomato is a food
    I'd certainly eschew.

It's best of all that everyone's
    So tolerant today
That I can write this sort of stuff
    And not get put away.

William Cole

RABBIT

A rabbit raced a turtle,
You know the turtle won;
And Mister Bunny came in late,
A little hot cross bun!

anon

Sally Arkari isn't she a treat
Bouncing her rubber ball
Up and down the street
Sticking plaster spectacles
Braces on her teeth
Always scoffing chocolates
Always crunching sweets
Never stops bouncing
Wherever she goes
Never stops sniffing
Never blows her nose
She bounces when she's laughing
She bounces when she weeps
She bounces when she's wide awake
She bounces when she sleeps
She bounces in the playground
She bounces in the hall
You can always tell it's Sally
By her bouncing rubber ball
She bounces during Geography
She bounces during Art
She bounces all through dinner time
In the custard tart
She bounces 'till she's out of breath
And her face turns red
She bounces in assembly
On the teacher's head
She bounces to the fairground
And makes the people cross
As she bounces in the fish and chips
And in the candy floss

She bounces into Paris
And for almost an hour
She bounced her little rubber ball
On the Eiffel tower
She bounced down to the circus
And up the greasy pole
She bounced down to the football ground
And bounced into the goal
She bounced beside the brass band
As it marched around the town
She bounced among the drummer boys
And made them all fall down
She bounced it on her knee caps
She bounced it on her head
Then she bounced her way back home again
And bounced into her bed.

Gareth Owen

AS I WAS GOING OUT ONE DAY

As I was going out one day
My head fell off and rolled away.
But when I saw that it was gone,
I picked it up and put it on.

And when I got into the street
A fellow cried: 'Look at your feet!'
I looked at them and sadly said:
'I've left them both asleep in bed!'

anon

AS I WAS COMING DOWN THE STAIR

As I was coming down the stair
I met a man who wasn't there;
He wasn't there again to-day:
I *wish* that man would go away.

anon

IF THE BUTTERFLY COURTED THE BEE

If the butterfly courted the bee,
    And the owl the porcupine;
If churches were built in the sea,
    And three times one was nine;
If the pony rode his master,
    If buttercups ate the cows,
If the cat had the dire disaster
    To be worried, sir, by the mouse;
If mamma, sir, sold the baby
    To the gipsy for half a crown;
If a gentleman, sir, was a lady –
    The world would be Upside-Down!
If any or all these wonders
    Should ever come about,
I should not consider them blunders,
    For I should be Inside-Out!

William Brighty Rands

SIX LITTLE MICE SAT DOWN TO SPIN

Six little mice sat down to spin;
Pussy passed by, and she peeped in.
'What are you doing, my little men?'
'Making coats for gentlemen.'
'Shall I come in and cut off your threads?'
'Oh no, Mistress Pussy, you'd bite off our
heads!'

anon

TO THE MOON

O Moon! when I look on your beautiful face
Careering along through the darkness of
    space,
The thought has quite frequently come to
    my mind
If ever I'll gaze on your lovely behind.

anon

HUMPTY DUMPTY'S POEM

In winter, when the fields are white,
I sing this song for your delight –

In spring, when woods are getting green,
I'll try and tell you what I mean.

In summer, when the days are long,
Perhaps you'll understand the song:

In autumn, when the leaves are brown,
Take pen and ink, and write it down.

I sent a message to the fish:
I told them 'This is what I wish.'

The little fishes of the sea,
Then sent an answer back to me.

The little fishes' answer was
'We cannot do it, Sir, because –'

I sent to them again to say
'It will be better to obey.'

The fishes answered with a grin,
'Why, what a temper you are in!'

I told them once, I told them twice:
They would not listen to advice.

I took a kettle large and new,
Fit for the deed I had to do.

My heart went hop, my heart went thump:
I filled the kettle at the pump.

Then someone came to me and said,
'The little fishes are in bed.'

I said to him, I said it plain,
'Then you must wake them up again.'

I said it very loud and clear;
I went and shouted in his ear.

But he was very stiff and proud;
He said, 'You needn't shout so loud!'

And he was very proud and stiff;
He said, 'I'd go and wake them, if –'

I took a corkscrew from the shelf:
I went to wake them up myself.

And when I found the door was locked,
I pulled and pushed and kicked and
knocked.

And when I found the door was shut,
I tried to turn the handle, but –

Lewis Carroll

DON'T WORRY IF YOUR JOB IS SMALL

Don't worry if your job is small,
And your rewards are few.
Remember that the mighty oak,
Was once a nut like you.

anon

'Quack!' said the billy-goat,
  'Oink!' said the hen.
'Miaow!' said the little chick
  Running in the pen.

'Hobble-gobble!' said the dog.
  'Cluck!' said the sow.
'Tu-whit tu-whoo!' the donkey said.
  'Baa!' said the cow.

'Hee-haw!' the turkey cried.
  The duck began to moo.
All at once the sheep went,
  'Cock-a-doodle-doo!'

The owl coughed and cleared his throat
  And he began to bleat.
'Bow-wow!' said the cock
  Swimming in the leat.

'Cheep-cheep!' said the cat
  As she began to fly.
'Farmer's been and laid an egg –
  That's the reason why.'

Charles Causley

WHEN FISHES SET UMBRELLAS UP

When fishes set umbrellas up
   If the rain-drops run,
Lizards will want their parasols
   To shade them from the sun.

The peacock has a score of eyes,
   With which he cannot see;
The cod-fish has a silent sound,
   However that may be.

No dandelions tell the time,
   Although they turn to clocks;
Cat's cradle does not hold the cat,
   Nor foxglove fit the fox.

Christina Rossetti

A DISSERTATION ON THE ANTIQUITY OF FLEAS

Adam
Had'em

anon

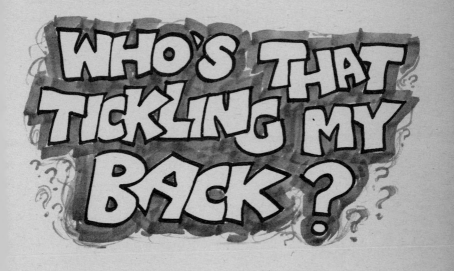

THE TICKLE RHYME

'Who's that tickling my back?' said the wall.
'Me,' said a small
Caterpillar. 'I'm learning
To crawl.'

Ian Serraillier

THE ANT

The ant has made himself illustrious
Through constant industry industrious.
So what?
Would you be calm and placid
If you were full of formic acid?

Ogden Nash

98

ANTS, ALTHOUGH ADMIRABLE,
ARE AWFULLY AGGRAVATING

The busy ant works hard all day
And never stops to rest or play.
He carries things ten times his size,
And never grumbles, whines or cries.
And even climbing flower stalks,
He always runs, he never walks.
He loves his work, he never tires,
And never puffs, pants or perspires.

Yet though I praise his boundless vim
I am not really fond of him.

Walter R. Brooks

THE SPIDER

How doth the jolly little spider
Wind up such miles of silk inside her?
The explanation seems to be
She does not eat so much as me.

And if I never, never cram
Myself with ginger-bread and jam,
Then maybe I'll have room to hide
A little rope in *my* inside.

Then I shall tie it very tight
Just over the electric light,
And hang head downward from the ceiling –
I wonder if one *minds* the feeling?

Or else I'd tie it to a tree
And let myself into the sea;
But when I wound it up again
I wonder if I'd have a pain?

A. P. Herbert

GULP!

CROSSING THE ROAD

Snails are not the friendly creatures
people might suppose,
they never stop to have a chat
when they meet nose to nose,
for
conversation-wise
it seems,
they don't have much to say
and vaguely waving horns around
continue
   on their way.

I'm cultivating two or three
and hoping that they'll talk
             to me.

Peggy Dunstan

BEES

Honeybees are very tricky –
Honey doesn't make them sticky.

Russell Hoban

Furry and Feathered Farmyard Friends

THE PIG

The pig, if I am not mistaken,
Supplies us with sausage, ham and bacon.
Let others say his heart is big –
I call it stupid of the pig.

Ogden Nash

THE PURPLE COW

I never saw a Purple Cow,
   I never hope to see one;
But I can tell you anyhow,
   I'd rather see than be one.

Gelett Burgess

ROOSTER

The rooster's
crowing
in the morning
is just his
silly way
of yawning.

N M Bodecker

THE COW

The cow is of the bovine ilk;
One end is moo, the other, milk.

Ogden Nash

WHY DO SHEEP

Why do sheep
have curly coats?

To keep the wind
out of their froats

Roger McGough

WILD ANIMALS AND CRAZY CREATURES

KANGAROO – KANGAROO!

The kangaroo of Australia
Lives on the burning plain,
He keeps on leaping in the air
'Cos it's hot when he lands again.

Spike Milligan

THE POLAR BEAR

A polar bear who could not spell
Sat worrying in the snow.
'I wish,' he said, 'that I could tell
If *flow* is right, or *floe*.'
But as he worried up there came
A hungry Eskimo
Who shot him and – it seems a shame –
That bear will never knoe.

Edward Lucie-Smith

THE FOUR FRIENDS

Ernest was an elephant, a great big fellow,
   Leonard was a lion with a six-foot tail,
George was a goat, and his beard was yellow,
     And James was a very small snail.

Leonard had a stall, and a great big strong
one,
   Ernest had a manger, and its walls were
thick,
George found a pen, but I think it was the
wrong one,
     And James sat down on a brick.

Ernest started trumpeting, and cracked his
manger.
   Leonard started roaring, and shivered his
stall.
James gave the huffle of a snail in danger,
     And nobody heard him at all.

Ernest started trumpeting and raised such a
rumpus,
   Leonard started roaring and trying to
kick,
James went a journey with the goat's new
compass
     And he reached the end of his brick.

Ernest was an elephant and very well-
intentioned,
     Leonard was a lion with a brave new tail,
George was a goat, as I think I have
mentioned,
     But James was only a snail.

A. A. Milne

THE VULTURE

The Vulture eats between his meals,
     And that's the reason why

He very, very rarely feels
     As well as you and I.
His eye is dull, his head is bald,
     His neck is growing thinner.
Oh! what a lesson for us all
     To only eat at dinner!

Hilaire Belloc

WARTHOG

Oh! to be a warthog
And bound about the plain.
To talk to other warthogs
Is not to live in vain.

Pixie O'Harris

THE PELICAN

What a wonderful beast is the Pelican!
Whose bill can hold more than his belican.
   He can take in his beak
   Enough food for a week –
           And I'm damned
        if I know
   how the helican.

anon

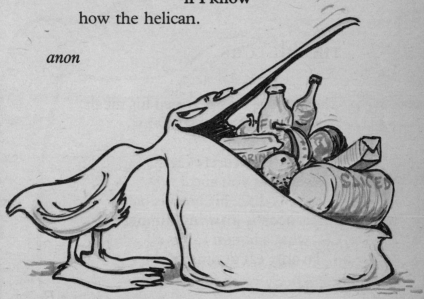

THE OSTRICH

The ostrich roams the great Sahara.
Its mouth is wide, its neck is narra.
It has such long and lofty legs,
I'm glad it sits to lay its eggs.

Ogden Nash

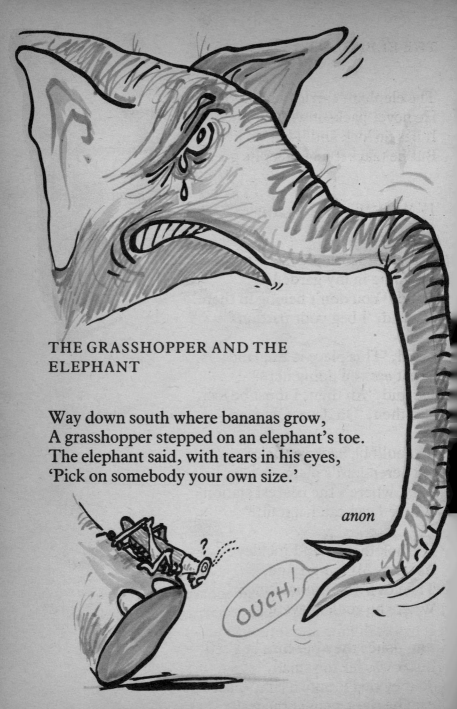

THE GRASSHOPPER AND THE ELEPHANT

Way down south where bananas grow,
A grasshopper stepped on an elephant's toe.
The elephant said, with tears in his eyes,
'Pick on somebody your own size.'

anon

OUCH!

THE ELEPHANT

The elephant carries a great big trunk;
He never packs it with clothes;
It has no lock and it has no key,
But he takes it wherever he goes.

anon

JUMBO-JET

I saw a little Elephant
Standing in my garden.
I said, 'You don't belong in there!'
He said, 'I beg your pardon.'

I said, 'This place is England,
What *are* you doing here?'
He said, 'Ah then, I must be lost,'
and then, 'Oh dear, Oh dear.'

'I should be back in Africa
On Serengetti's plain.
Pray, where's the nearest station
Where I can catch a train?'

He took the bus to Finchley
As far as Mincing Lane,
Then over the Embankment,
Where he got lost again.

The police they put him in a cell
But it was far too small,
So they tied him to a lamp-post
And he slept against the wall.

But as the policemen lay in bed
By the tinkling light of dawn,
The lamp-post and the wall were there
But the Elephant was gone.

So if you see an Elephant
In a Jumbo-Jet,
You can be sure that Africa,
Is the place he's trying to get.

Spike Milligan

GIRAFFE

I like
giraffe
and hope that he
in his
own way
is fond of me,

despite
the fact
that he and I
did never
quite
see eye to eye.

N. M. Bodecker

THE COMMON CORMORANT

The common cormorant or shag
Lays eggs inside a paper bag
The reason you will see no doubt
It is to keep the lightning out.
But what these unobservant birds
Have never noticed is that herds
Of wandering bears may come with buns
And steal the bags to hold the crumbs.

anon

THE HIPPOPOTAMUS

I shoot the Hippopotamus
    with bullets made of platinum,
Because if I used leaden ones
    his hide is sure to flatten 'em.

Hilaire Belloc

DANGERS OF THE DEEP

TONY THE TURTLE

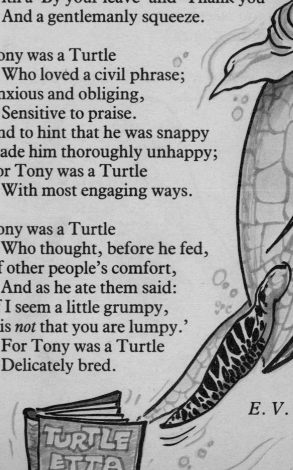

Tony was a Turtle,
  Very much at ease,
Swimming in the sunshine
  Through the summer seas,
And feeding on the fishes
Irrespective of their wishes,
With a 'By your leave' and 'Thank you'
  And a gentlemanly squeeze.

Tony was a Turtle
  Who loved a civil phrase;
Anxious and obliging,
  Sensitive to praise.
And to hint that he was snappy
Made him thoroughly unhappy;
For Tony was a Turtle
  With most engaging ways.

Tony was a Turtle
  Who thought, before he fed,
Of other people's comfort,
  And as he ate them said:
'If I seem a little grumpy,
It is *not* that you are lumpy.'
  For Tony was a Turtle
  Delicately bred.

E. V. Rieu

IF YOU SHOULD MEET A
CROCODILE...

If you should meet a crocodile,
  Don't take a stick and poke him;
Ignore the welcome in his smile,
  Be careful not to stroke him.
For as he sleeps upon the Nile,
  He thinner gets and thinner;
And whene'er you meet a crocodile
  He's ready for his dinner.

anon

HOW DOTH THE LITTLE CROCODILE

How doth the little crocodile
   Improve his shining tail,
And pour the waters of the Nile
   On every golden scale!

How cheerfully he seems to grin,
   How neatly spreads his claws,
And welcomes little fishes in,
   With gently smiling jaws!

Lewis Carroll

Said the Shark to the Flying-Fish over the
    phone:
'Will you join me to-night? I am dining
    alone.
Let me order a nice little dinner for two!
And come as you are, in your shimmering
    blue.'

Said the Flying-Fish: 'Fancy remembering
    me,
And the dress that I wore at the Porpoises'
    tea!'
'How could I forget?' said the Shark in his
    guile:
'I expect you at eight!' and rang off with a
    smile.

She has powdered her nose; she has put on
    her things;
She is off with one flap of her luminous
    wings.
O little one, lovely, light-hearted and vain,
The Moon will not shine on your beauty
    again!

E. V. Rieu

THE COD

There's something very strange and odd
About the habits of the Cod.

For when you're swimming in the sea,
He sometimes bites you on the knee.

And though his bites are not past healing,
It is a most unpleasant feeling.

And when you're diving down below,
He often nips you on the toe.

And though he doesn't hurt you much,
He has a disagreeable touch.

There's one thing to be said for him, –
It is a treat to see him swim.

But though he swims in graceful curves,
He rather gets upon your nerves.

Lord Alfred Douglas

THE SEA

The place for me,
Is not the sea.

I might sink,
I think.

Another thing,
Jellyfish sting.

Crabs have claws,
Sharks have jaws.

In the sun,
The waves look fun.

But underneath,
The horrible teeth.

Gregory Allin, 15

IT MAKES A CHANGE

There's nothing makes a Greenland Whale
Feel half so high-and-mighty,
As sitting on a mantelpiece
In Aunty Mabel's nighty.

It makes a change from Freezing Seas,
(Of which a Whale can tire),
To warm his weary tail at ease
Before an English fire.

For this delight he leaves the sea,
(Unknown to Aunty Mabel),
Returning only when the dawn
Lights up the Breakfast Table.

Mervyn Peake

WISE WARNINGS, BEASTLY BEHAVIOUR AND AWFUL ENDS

LITTLE CLOTILDA

Little Clotilda,
Well and hearty,
Thought she'd like
To give a party.
But as her friends
Were shy and wary,
Nobody came
But her own canary.

anon

THE HOUSE ON THE HILL

It was built years ago
by someone quite manic
and sends those who go there
away in blind panic.
They tell tales of horrors
that can injure or kill
designed by the madman
who lived on the hill.

If you visit the House on the Hill for a dare
remember my words . . .
'There are dangers. Beware!'

The piano's white teeth
when you plonk out a note
will bite off your fingers
then reach for your throat.
The living room curtains
– long, heavy and black –
will wrap you in cobwebs
if you're slow to step back.

If you enter the House on the Hill for a dare
remember my words . . .
'There are dangers. Beware!'

The 'fridge in the kitchen
has a self-closing door.
If it knocks you inside
then you're ice cubes . . . for sure.
The steps to the cellar
are littered with bones,
and up from the darkness
drift creakings and groans.

If you go to the House on the Hill for a dare
remember my words . . .
                    'There are dangers. Beware!'

Turn on the hot tap
and the bathroom will flood
not with gallons of water
but litres of blood.
The rocking-chair's arms
can squeeze you to death;
a waste of time shouting
as you run . . . out . . . of . . . breath.

Don't say you weren't warned or told to
take care
when you entered the House on the Hill . . .
                            for a dare.

Wes Magee

I SAW A JOLLY HUNTER

I saw a jolly hunter
   With a jolly gun
Walking in the country
   In the jolly sun.

In the jolly meadow
   Sat a jolly hare.
Saw the jolly hunter.
   Took jolly care.

Hunter jolly eager –
  Sight of jolly prey.
Forgot gun pointing
  Wrong jolly way.

Jolly hunter jolly head
  Over heels gone.
Jolly old safety-catch
  Not jolly on.

Bang went the jolly gun.
  Hunter jolly dead.
Jolly hare got clean away.
  Jolly good, I said.

Charles Causley

137

MISGUIDED MARCUS

Marcus met an alligator
Half a mile from the equator;
Marcus, ever optimistic,
Said, 'This beast is not sadistic.'
Marcus even claimed the creature
'Has a kind and loving nature'.
In that case, pray tell me, Marcus,
Why have you become a carcass?

Colin West

THE BOY STOOD IN THE SUPPER-ROOM

The boy stood in the supper-room
   Whence all but he had fled;
He'd eaten seven pots of jam
   And he was gorged with bread.

'Oh, one more crust before I bust!'
   He cried in accents wild;
He licked the plates, he sucked the spoons –
   He was a vulgar child.

There came a burst of thunder-sound –
   The boy – oh! where was he?
Ask of the maid who mopped him up,
   The bread crumbs and the tea!

anon

TWICKENHAM

There was a young lady of Twickenham,
Whose boots were too tight to walk
  quickenham.
      She bore them awhile,
      But at last, at a stile,
She pulled them both off and was
  sickenham.

anon

HENRY KING

Who chewed bits of String, and was early cut off in
Dreadful Agonies.

The chief defect of Henry King
Was chewing little bits of String.
At last he swallowed some which tied
Itself in ugly Knots inside.

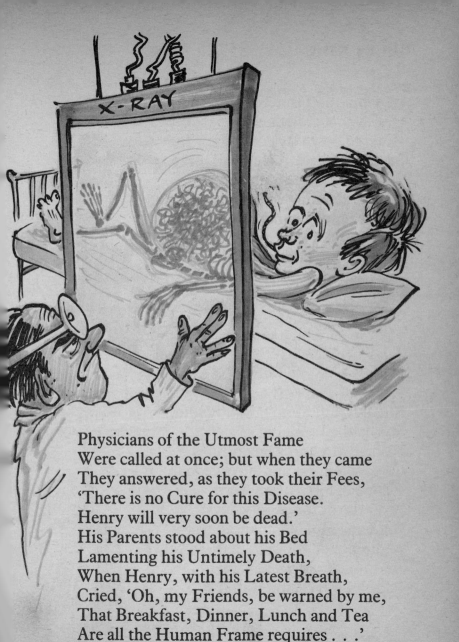

Physicians of the Utmost Fame
Were called at once; but when they came
They answered, as they took their Fees,
'There is no Cure for this Disease.
Henry will very soon be dead.'
His Parents stood about his Bed
Lamenting his Untimely Death,
When Henry, with his Latest Breath,
Cried, 'Oh, my Friends, be warned by me,
That Breakfast, Dinner, Lunch and Tea
Are all the Human Frame requires . . .'
With that the Wretched Child expires.

Hilaire Belloc

Jelly Jake and Butter Bill
One dark night when all was still
Pattered down the long, dark stair,
And no one saw the guilty pair;
Pushed aside the pantry-door
And there found everything galore, –
Honey, raisins, orange-peel,
Cold chicken aplenty for a meal,
Gingerbread enough to fill
Two such boys as Jake and Bill.
Well, they ate and ate and ate,
Gobbled at an awful rate
Till I'm sure they soon weighed more
Than double what they did before.
And then, it's awful, still it's true,
The floor gave way and they went through.
Filled so full they couldn't fight,
Slowly they sank out of sight.
Father, Mother, Cousin Ann,
Cook and nurse and furnace man
Fished in forty-dozen ways
After them, for twenty days;
But not a soul has chanced to get
A glimpse or glimmer of them yet.
And I'm afraid we never will –
Poor Jelly Jake and Butter Bill.

Leroy Jackson

THE CURE

'I've swallowed a fly,' cried Marjorie Fry.
  (We could hear it buzzing inside her.)
'And I haven't a hope of getting it out
  Unless I swallow a spider.'

We found a web by the garden wall,
  And back to the house we hurried
And offered the spider to Marjorie Fry,
  Who was looking extremely worried.

'Now shut your eyelids, Marjorie Fry,
  And open your wee mouth wider. ·
Whatever it does, the fly won't buzz
  If only you'll swallow the spider.'

Alfred Noyes

WINDY

The gale upon our holidays
Was not your passing breeze.
It gave our tents a fearful wrench
And bent the frantic trees.
So, if you've seen a flying tent,
And then observe another,
Please call us at your earliest,
We're also missing mother.

Max Fatchen

Isabel met an enormous bear;
Isabel, Isabel, didn't care.
The bear was hungry, the bear was ravenous,
The bear's big mouth was cruel and
    cavernous.

The bear said, Isabel, glad to meet you,
How do, Isabel, now I'll eat you!
Isabel, Isabel, didn't worry;
Isabel didn't scream or scurry.
She washed her hands and she straightened
    her hair up,
Then Isabel quietly ate the bear up.

Ogden Nash

Mr Hector Pennycomequick
   Stood on the castle keep,
Opened up a carriage-umbrella
   And took a mighty leap.

'Hooray!' cried Mr Pennycomequick
   As he went through the air.
'I've always wanted to go like this
   From here to Newport Square.'

But Mr Hector Pennycomequick
   He never did float nor fly.
He landed in an ivy-bush,
   His legs up in the sky.

Mr Hector Pennycomequick
   They hurried home to bed
With a bump the size of a sea-gull's egg
   On the top of his head.

'So sorry,' said Mr Pennycomequick,
   'For causing all this fuss.
When next I go to Newport Square
   I think I'll take the bus.'

The moral of this little tale
   Is difficult to refute:
A carriage-umbrella's a carriage-umbrella
   And not a parachute.

Charles Causley

TWICKHAM TWEER

Shed a tear for Twickham Tweer
who ate uncommon meals,
who often peeled bananas
and then only ate the peels,
who emptied jars of marmalade
and only ate the jars,
and only ate the wrappers
off of chocolate candy bars.

When Twickham cooked a chicken
he would only eat the bones,
he discarded scoops of ice cream
though he always ate the cones,
he'd boil a small potato
but he'd only eat the skin,
and pass up canned asparagus
to gobble down the tin.

He sometimes dined on apple cores
and bags of peanut shells,
on cottage cheese containers,
cellophane from caramels,
but Twickham Tweer passed on last year,
that odd and novel man,
when he fried an egg one morning
and then ate the frying pan.

Jack Prelutsky

MATILDA

Who told Lies, and was Burned to Death

Matilda told such dreadful lies,
It made one gasp and stretch one's eyes;
Her Aunt, who, from her earliest youth,
Had kept a strict regard for truth,
Attempted to believe Matilda:
The effort very nearly killed her,
And would have done so, had not she
Discovered this infirmity.
For once, towards the close of day,
Matilda, growing tired of play,
And finding she was left alone,
Went tiptoe to the telephone
And summoned the immediate aid
Of London's noble fire-brigade.

Within an hour the gallant band
Were pouring in on every hand,
From Putney, Hackney Downs, and Bow
With courage high and hearts a-glow
They galloped, roaring through the town,
'Matilda's house is burning down!'
Inspired by British cheers and loud
Proceeding from the frenzied crowd,
They ran their ladders through a score
Of windows on the ballroom floor;
And took peculiar pains to souse
The pictures up and down the house,
Until Matilda's Aunt succeeded
In showing them they were not needed;
And even then she had to pay
To get the men to go away!

It happened that a few weeks later
Her Aunt was off to the theatre
To see that interesting play
The Second Mrs Tanqueray,
She had refused to take her niece
To hear this entertaining piece:
A deprivation just and wise
To punish her for telling lies.
That night a fire *did* break out –
You should have heard Matilda shout!
You should have heard her scream and bawl,
And throw the window up and call
To people passing in the street –

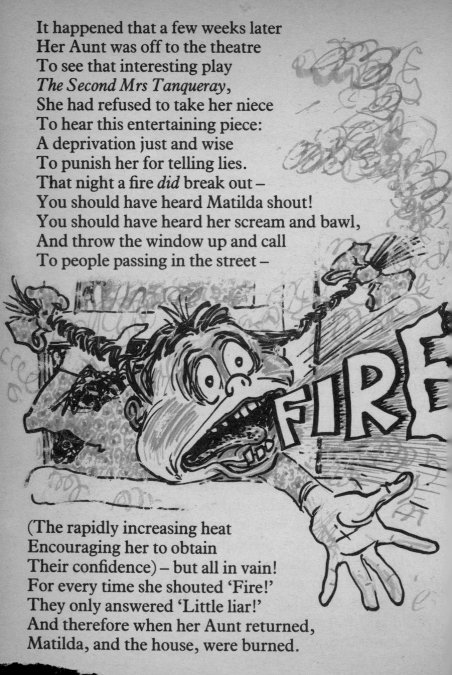

(The rapidly increasing heat
Encouraging her to obtain
Their confidence) – but all in vain!
For every time she shouted 'Fire!'
They only answered 'Little liar!'
And therefore when her Aunt returned,
Matilda, and the house, were burned.

Hilaire Belloc

KENNETH
who was too fond of bubble-gum and met an
untimely end

The chief defect of Kenneth Plumb
Was chewing too much bubble-gum.
He chewed away with all his might,
Morning, evening, noon and night.
Even (oh, it makes you weep)
Blowing bubbles in his sleep.
He simply couldn't get enough!
His face was covered with the stuff.
As for his teeth – oh, what a sight!
It was a wonder he could bite.
His loving mother and his dad
Both remonstrated with the lad.
Ken repaid them for the trouble
By blowing yet another bubble.

Twas no joke. It isn't funny
Spending all your pocket money
On the day's supply of gum –
Sometimes Kenny felt quite glum.
As he grew, so did his need –
There seemed no limit to his greed:
At ten he often put away
Ninety seven packs a day.

Then at last he went too far –
Sitting in his father's car,
Stuffing gum without a pause,
Found that he had jammed his jaws.
He nudged his dad and pointed to
The mouthful that he couldn't chew.

'Well, spit it out if you can't chew it!'
Ken shook his head. He couldn't do it.
Before long he began to groan –
The gum was solid as a stone.
Dad took him to a builder's yard;
They couldn't help. It was too hard.
They called a doctor and he said,
'This silly boy will soon be dead.
His mouth's so full of bubble-gum
No nourishment can reach his tum.'

Remember Ken and please do not
Go buying too much you-know-what.

Wendy Cope

THE HEADLESS GARDENER

A gardener, Tobias Baird,
Sent his head to be repaired;
He thought, as nothing much was wrong,
He wouldn't be without it long.

Ten years he's weeded path and plot,
A headless gardener, God wot,
Always hoping (hope is vain)
To see his noddle back again.

Don't pity him for his distress –
He never sent up his address.

Ian Serraillier

POLITENESS

If people ask me,
I always tell them:
'Quite well, thank you, I'm very glad to say.'
If people ask me,
I always answer,
'Quite well, thank you, how are you to-day?'
I always answer,
I always tell them,
If they ask me
Politely . . .

BUT SOMETIMES

I wish

That they wouldn't.

A. A. Milne

POLITENESS BE SUGARED, POLITENESS BE HANGED

'Politeness be sugared, politeness be hanged,
Politeness be jumbled and tumbled and
    banged.
It's simply a matter of putting on pace,
Politeness has nothing to do with the case.'

Norman Lindsay

LITTLE BILLEE

There were three sailors of Bristol city
Who took a boat and went to sea,
But first with beef and captain's biscuits
And pickled pork they loaded she.

There was gorging Jack and guzzling Jimmy
And the youngest he was little Billee.
Now when they had got as far as the Equator
They'd nothing left but one split pea.

Says gorging Jack to guzzling Jimmy,
'I am extremely hungaree.'
To gorging Jack says guzzling Jimmy,
'We've nothing left, us must eat we.'

Says gorging Jack to guzzling Jimmy,
'With one another we shouldn't agree!
There's little Bill, he's young and tender,
We're old and tough, so let's eat he.'

'Oh! Billee, we're going to kill and eat you
So undo the button of your chemie.'
When Bill received this information
He used his pocket handkerchie.

'First let me say my catechism,
Which my poor mammy taught to me.'
'Make haste, make haste,' says guzzling
    Jimmy,
While Jack pulled out his snickersnee.

So Billee went up to the main top gallant
   mast,
And down he fell on his bended knee.
He scarce had come to the twelfth
   commandment
When up he jumps, 'There's land I see:

'Jerusalem and Madagascar,
And North and South Amerikee:
There's a British flag a-riding at anchor,
With Admiral Napier, K.C.B.'

So when they got aboard of the Admiral's,
He hanged fat Jack and flogged Jimmee:
But as for little Bill he made him
The Captain of a Seventy-three.

W. M. Thackeray

TENDER-HEARTEDNESS

Billy, in one of his nice new sashes,
Fell in the fire and was burned to ashes;
Now, although the room grows chilly,
I haven't the heart to poke poor Billy.

Harry Graham

MALCOLM

Let us pray for cousin Malcolm,
Smothered as he was in talcum;
He sneezed whilst seasoning his chowder
And vanished in a puff of powder.

Colin West

EPITAPH TO A DENTIST

Stranger! Approach this spot with gravity!
John Brown is filling his last cavity.

anon

WORD OF HONOUR

No power of language can express
The irritation and distress
   It used to be to Mrs Trales
   To see her children bite their nails.

In vain she tied their hands in bags:
They chewed the corners into rags.
   Even bitter aloes proved a waste:
   The children grew to like the taste.

So for a week with constant smacks
She bound their hands behind their backs:
   Then said, 'Now promise, George and
     Jane,
   Never to bite your nails again!'

And when the promise had been wrung
From sobbing throat and stammering
     tongue,
   She added, with a threatening brow,
   'Mind! You're upon your honour now!'

The votive pair, their spirits bowed,
With sullen looks the claim allowed;
   And 'bound in honour' forth they went
   To try a fresh experiment.

Time passed: till Mrs Trales one day
Remarked in quite a casual way –
   Threading her needle in between –
   'Come, show me if your hands are clean!'

With conscious looks the guilty pair
   Adjusted flattened palms in air:
   But she, not meaning to be lax,
   Observed, 'Now let me see the backs!'

Which being shown, there plain to see
Were nails as short as short could be!
   'What!' cried Mamma, her anger stirred,
   'Is this the way you keep your word?'

Then, nerved to desperation, Jane
Cried, 'Wait, Mamma, and I'll explain:
   For bad at first though things appear,
   Indeed it is not as you fear!

'Though at first glance our nails may strike
Your eye as shorter than you'd like,
   Yet, dear Mamma, pray bear in mind
   For weeks they have been much behind!

'And often, when the wish occurred
To bite them, we recalled our word,
   And never, never would we break
   The promise we were forced to make!

'So, now, whenever George or I
Starve for a taste of finger-pie,
   Then turn and turn about we dine –
   First I bite his, then he bites mine.'

What happened next you may surmise,
While in between came anguished cries –
   'You never did put me or Brother
   On honour not to bite each other!'

Laurence Houseman

THERE WAS A YOUNG LADY OF RIGA

There was a Young Lady of Riga
Who rode with a smile on a tiger;
   They returned from the ride
   With the lady inside,
And the smile on the face of the tiger.

anon

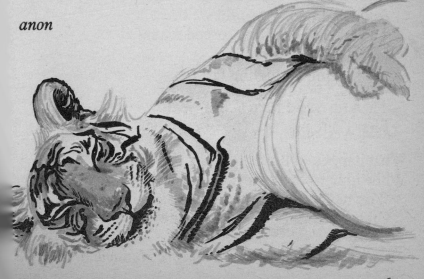

THE BOY

The boy stood on the burning deck,
His feet were full of blisters;
The flames came up and burned his pants,
And now he wears his sister's.

anon

STORYTIME

Once upon a time, children,
there lived a fearsome dragon . . .

Please, miss,
Jamie's made a dragon.
Out in the sandpit.

Lovely, Andrew.
Now this dragon
had enormous red eyes
and a swirling, whirling tail . . .

Jamie's dragon's got
yellow eyes, miss.

Lovely, Andrew.
Now this dragon was
as wide as a horse
as green as the grass
as tall as a house . . .

162

*Jamie's would JUST fit
in our classroom, miss!*

But he was a very friendly dragon . . .

*Jamie's dragon ISN'T, miss.
He eats people, miss.
Especially TEACHERS,
Jamie said.*

Very nice, Andrew!

Now one day, children,
this enormous dragon
rolled his red eye,
whirled his swirly green tail
and set off to find . . .

*His dinner, miss!
Because he was hungry, miss!*

Thank you, Andrew.
He rolled his red eye,
whirled his green tail,
and opened his wide, wide mouth
until

*Please, miss,
I did try to tell you, miss!*

Judith Nicholls

ON A BAD SINGER

Swans sing before they die – 'twere no bad
   thing
Should certain persons die before they sing.

Samuel Taylor Coleridge

JOHN BUN

Here lies John Bun,
He was killed by a gun,
His name was not Bun, but Wood,
But Wood would not rhyme with gun, but
Bun would.

anon

JIMMY JUPP, WHO DIED OF OVER-EATING

Oh, shed no tears for Jimmy Jupp;
He was a most revolting pup:
He sucked his teeth, he picked his nose,
He bit his nails, he scratched his toes;
At parties he would sit and stuff,
And never seemed to have enough
Of turkey, pies and Christmas pud
Which, in excess, are not too good.
One night he ate so many pies
He swelled to an enormous size.
In spite of this he would not stop
Until, at last, he went off POP!

His friends remarked, 'It might be wuss.
At least, there'll now be more for us!'

H. A. C. Evans

FOOLISH FOLKS AND FUNNY FELLOWS

NERO

Nero, plump about the middle,
Played requests upon the fiddle.
The most engaging tune he played
Was for the local fire brigade.

Colin West

EDWARD THE CONFESSOR

Edward the Confessor
Slept under the dresser.
When that began to pall,
He slept in the hall.

E. Clerihew Bentley

KING FOO FOO

King Foo Foo sat upon his throne
Dressed in his royal closes,
While all round his courtiers stood
With clothes-pegs on their noses.

'This action strange,' King Foo Foo said,
'My mind quite discomposes,
Though vulgar curiosity
A good king never shoses.'

But to the court it was as clear
As poetry or prose is:
King Foo Foo had not had a bath
Since goodness only knoses.

But one fine day the Fire Brigade
Rehearsing with their hoses
(To Handel's 'Water Music' played
With many puffs and bloses)

Quite failed the water to control
In all its ebbs and floses
And simply drenched the King with sev-
Eral thousand gallon doses.

At this each wight (though impolite)
A mighty grin exposes.
'At last,' the King said, 'now I see
That all my court morose is!

'A debt to keep his courtiers gay
A monarch surely owses,
And deep within my royal breast
A sporting heart reposes'.

So now each night its water bright
The Fire Brigade disposes
Over a King who smiles as sweet
As all the royal roses.

Charles Causley

MICHAEL

Michael likes 'Michael',
He doesn't like 'Mike'.
He rides on a 'cycle',
And *not* on a 'bike'.
He doesn't like 'Mickey',
He doesn't like 'Mick';
Don't offer a 'bikky' –
It might make him sick.

Colin West

CAPTAIN KIDD
1650?–1701

This person in the gaudy clothes
Is worthy Captain Kidd.
They say he never buried gold
I think, perhaps, he did.

They say it's all a story that
His favorite little song
Was 'Make these lubbers walk the plank!'
I think, perhaps, they're wrong.

They say he never pirated
Beneath the Skull-and-Bones.
He merely traveled for his health
And spoke in soothing tones.
In fact, you'll read in nearly all
The newer history books
That he was mild as cottage cheese
– *But I don't like his looks!*

Rosemary and Stephen Vincent Benet

There lived an Old Man in the Kingdom of
    Tess,
Who invented a purely original dress;
And when it was perfectly made and
    complete,
He opened the door, and walked into the
    street.

By way of a hat, he'd a loaf of Brown Bread,
In the middle of which he inserted his
    head; —
His Shirt was made up of no end of dead
    Mice,
The warmth of whose skins was quite fluffy
    and nice; —
His Drawers were of Rabbit-skins; — so were
    his Shoes; —
His Stockings were skins, — but it is not
    known whose; —
His Waistcoat and Trowsers were made of
    Pork Chops; —
His Buttons were Jujubes, and Chocolate
    Drops; —
His Coat was all Pancakes with Jam for a
    border,
And a girdle of Biscuits to keep it in order;

He had walked a short way, when he heard a
    great noise,
Of all sorts of Beasticles, Birdlings, and
    Boys; —

And from every long street and dark lane in
the town
Beasts, Birdles, and Boys in a tumult rushed
down.
Two Cows and a half ate his Cabbage-leaf
Cloak; –
Four Apes seized his Girdle, which vanished
like smoke;–
Three Kids ate up half of his Pancakey
Coat, –
And the tails were devour'd by an ancient
He-Goat; –
An army of Dogs in a twinkling tore *up* his
Pork Waistcoat and Trowsers to give to their
Puppies; –
And while they were growling, and
mumbling the Chops,
Ten Boys prigged the Jujubes and Chocolate
Drops. –

He tried to run back to his house, but in
vain,
For Scores of fat Pigs came again and
again; –
They rushed out of stables and hovels and
doors, –
They tore off his stockings, his shoes, and
his drawers, –
And now from the housetops with
screechings descend,
Striped, spotted, white, black, and gray Cats
without end,
They jumped on his shoulders and knocked
off his hat, –

When Crows, Ducks, and Hens made a
    mincemeat of that; –
They speedily flew at his sleeves in a trice,
And utterly tore up his Shirt of dead Mice; –
They swallowed the last of his Shirt with a
    squall, –
Whereon he ran home with no clothes on at
    all.

And he said to himself as he bolted the door,
'I will not wear a similar dress any more,
Any more, any more, any more, never
    more!'

Edward Lear

DIDDLING

    The people of Diddling
    Are never more than middling
For they can't abide either cold or heat.
    If the weather is damp,
    It gives them cramp,
And a touch of frost goes straight to their
    feet.

    A thundery shower
    Turns everything sour,
And a dry spell ruins the farmers' crops,
    And a south-west wind
    Is nobody's friend
For it blows the smoke down the chimney-
    tops.

Says old Mrs Morley,
'I'm middling poorly,
But thank you, I never was one to complain;
For the cold in my nose
As soon as it goes
I dursn't but say I may get it again.'

Old Grandfather Snell
Has never been well
Since he took to his crutches at seventy-
three;
And the elder Miss Lake
Has a travelling ache
Which finds its way down from her neck to
her knee.

The people of Diddling
Are never more than middling –
Not one but has headaches or palsy or gout.
But what they fear worst
Is a fine sunny burst,
For then there'll be nothing to grumble
about.

James Reeves

CROFT

Aloft,
In the loft,
Sits Croft;
He is soft.

Stevie Smith

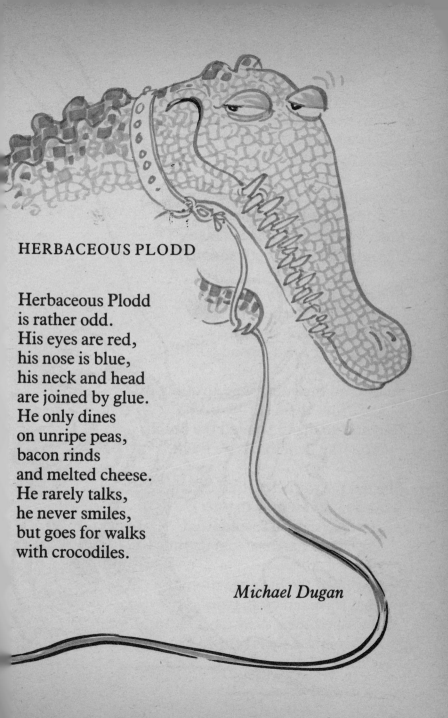

HERBACEOUS PLODD

Herbaceous Plodd
is rather odd.
His eyes are red,
his nose is blue,
his neck and head
are joined by glue.
He only dines
on unripe peas,
bacon rinds
and melted cheese.
He rarely talks,
he never smiles,
but goes for walks
with crocodiles.

Michael Dugan

THE CARES OF A CARETAKER

A nice old lady by the sea
   Was neat as she was plain,
And every time the tide came in
   She swept it back again.

And when the sea untidy grew
   And waves began to beat,
She took her little garden rake
   And raked it smooth and neat.

She ran a carpet-sweeper up
   And down the pebbly sand.
She said, 'This is the only way
   To keep it clean – good land!'

And when the gulls came strolling by,
   She drove them shrilly back,
Remarking that it spoiled the beach,
   'The way them birds do track.'

She fed the catfish clotted cream
   And taught it how to purr –
And were a catfish so endowed
   She would have stroked its fur.

She stopped the little sea urchins
   That travelled by in pairs,
And washed their dirty faces clean
   And combed their little hairs.

She spread white napkins on the surf
  With which she fumed and fussed.
'When it ain't covered up,' she said,
  'It gits all over dust.'

She didn't like to see the ships
  With all the waves act free,
And so she got a painted sign
  Which read: 'Keep off the Sea.'

But dust and splutter as she might,
  Her work was sadly vain;
However oft she swept the beach,
  The tides came in again.

And she was sometimes wan and worn
  When she retired to bed –
'A woman's work ain't never done,'
  That nice old lady said.

Wallace Irwin

LADIES OF OCEAN AVENUE

Ladies of Ocean Avenue
Devoid of humour, lacking hue,
Politely walk the Sunday Street
On pointed, thin, and boneless feet.
But ladies who live at Darlinghurst
Who dine on wine and liverwurst,
They stride the pavements in size seven,
And maybe, they are nearer Heaven.

Pixie O'Harris

DOCTOR BELL

Doctor Bell fell down the well
And broke his collar-bone.
Doctors should attend the sick
And leave the well alone.

anon

DO NOT WEAR A BROOM TO BREAKFAST

MISS NAN KNOCKABOUT

Miss Nan Knockabout
Wouldn't wash her face,
And everybody thought it was
A real disgrace.
Mud, soot and marmalade
Smeared her cheeks and chin,
You wouldn't have believed
She had a clean white skin.
One day the chimney sweep
Knocked on Nancy's door
And said, 'Little maiden, you're
the one that I adore.
Please say you'll marry me
And then we shall be
The finest pair o' chimney sweeps
You ever did see.'
But Miss Nan Knockabout
Screamed and ran away
And ordered twenty pounds of soap
that very same day.

Anon

Mum says things like
If you don't turn out your light . . .
If you don't eat your tea . . .
If you don't turn off TV . . .
If you don't dust for me . . .
If you don't drink your coffee . . .
Everyone says if you don't
I say I won't!

Dad says things like
If you don't stay in tonight . . .
If you don't stop arguing . . .
If you don't stop bickering . . .
If you don't go to bed . . .
If you don't do as I said . . .
Everyone says if you don't
I say I won't.

Brother says things like
If you don't play a game of tye . . .
If you don't play computer . . .
If you don't play snooker . . .
If you don't give me your sweets . . .
If you don't give me your seat . . .
Everyone says if you don't
I say I won't.

I say things like
If you don't lend me your bike . . .
If you don't teach me to knit . . .
If you don't stop being a twit . . .
If you don't let me get on . . .
If you don't stop singing songs . . .
I say if you don't
They say we won't.

Karen Parker (9)

ASK MUMMY, ASK DADDY

When I ask Daddy
Daddy says ask Mummy.

When I ask Mummy
Mummy says ask Daddy.
I don't know where to go.

Better ask my teddy.
He never says no.

John Agard

ADVICE

Do put a coat on,
and fasten that shoe.
I'd take a sweater,
    if I were you . . .

It's chilly at nights now,
you're bound to catch 'flu;
I'd button up warmly
    if I were you . . .

Please yourself if you must
but I know what *I'd* do;
I'd stay at home now,
    if I were you . . .

The nights have drawn in,
you never know who
might be lurking out there
    just waiting for you . . .

MUGGER
REPELLANT
D.I.Y. KIT.

I don't know what the youth
of today's coming to!
They do what they like
    and like what they do!

Now when *I* was young,
it caused hullaballoo
if I stayed out past nine –
    and I never dared to.

If I were young now,
I know what *I'd* do . . .

I'd enjoy every minute
    if I were you!

Judith Nicholls

RULES

Do not jump on ancient uncles.
*
Do not yell at average mice.
*
Do not wear a broom to breakfast.
*
Do not ask a snake's advice.
*
Do not bathe in chocolate pudding.
*
Do not talk to bearded bears.
*
Do not smoke cigars on sofas.
*
Do not dance on velvet chairs.
*
Do not take a whale to visit
Russell's mother's cousin's yacht.
*
And whatever else you do do
It is better you
Do not.

Karla Kuskin

ACKNOWLEDGEMENTS

The editor and publishers gratefully acknowledge permission to reproduce the following copyright material:

John Agard: 'Ask Mummy, Ask Daddy' from *I Din Do Nuttin & Other Poems* by John Agard, illustrated by Susanna Gretz. Reprinted by permission of The Bodley Head. Dorothy Aldis: 'My Nose' from *All Together* by Dorothy Aldis © 1967. Reprinted by permission of G. P. Putnam's Sons. Gregory Allin: 'The Sea' from *Words on Water*. Reprinted by permission of the author and Embrook School. Hilaire Belloc: 'Matilda' and 'Henry King' from *Cautionary Tales*; 'The Lion' and 'The Hippopotamus' from *The Bad Child's Book of Beasts*; 'The Vulture' from *More Beasts for Worse Children*. Reprinted by permission of Gerald Duckworth & Co. Ltd. John Betjeman: 'Hunter Trials' from *Collected Poems*. Reprinted by permission of John Murray (Publishers) Ltd. Carey Blyton: 'The Plughole Man' from *Bananas in Pyjamas*. Reprinted by permission of the author. N. M. Bodecker: 'Getting Together' from *Let's Marry, Said the Cherry* by N. M. Bodecker. Reprinted by permission of Faber & Faber Ltd. 'Rooster' and 'Giraffe' from *Snowman Snuffles & Other Verse* by N. M. Bodecker. Reprinted by permission of Faber & Faber Ltd. Alan Bold: 'The Caterpillar' from *Bright Lights Blaze Out* by Alan Bold, Julie O'Callaghan and Gareth Owen. Copyright © Alan Bold 1986. Reprinted by permission of Oxford University Press. Keith Bosley: 'The Fastest Train in the World' from *And I Dance* by Keith Bosley. Reprinted with permission of Angus & Robertson Publishers. Walter R. Brooks: 'Ants, Although Admirable . . .' from *The Walker Book of Poetry*, selected by Jack Prelutsky, published by Walker Books Ltd. Reprinted by permission of Walker Books Ltd. Charles Causley: 'I Saw a Jolly Hunter' from *Collected Poems 1951–1975*, published by Macmillan; 'Mr Pennycomequick', '"Quack!" said the Billy-Goat' and 'King Foo Foo' from *Figgie Hobbin*, published by Macmillan. Reprinted by permission of David Higham Associates Ltd. William Cole: 'A Song of Thanks' from *A Boy Named Mary Jane* © 1977 William Cole. Reprinted by permission of the author. Wendy Cope: 'Kenneth' from *Uncollected Poems*. Reprinted by permission of the author and Faber & Faber Ltd. Mary Dawson: 'Late for Breakfast' from *Allsorts 2* by Ann Thwaite. Reprinted by permission of Macmillan London & Basingstoke. Lord Alfred Douglas: 'The Cod' from *Tales with a Twist* by Lord Alfred Douglas © Edward Colman, the Douglas Literary Estate. Reprinted by permission of B. T. Batsford Ltd. Michael Dugan: 'Herbaceous Plodd' from *Wotcha-ma-callit Annual*, edited by P. Viska, published by *Sunday Observer*, Melbourne, 1974, and 'My Uncle Robert' from *Someone is Flying Balloons*, compiled by J. Heylen and C. Jellett, published by Omnibus Books, Adelaide, 1983. Reprinted by permission of Michael Dugan. Peggy Dunstan: 'Crossing the Road' from *In and Out the Windows*. Reprinted by permission of Hodder & Stoughton Ltd, New Zealand. Gavin Ewart: 'Never Try to Make Your Meals' and 'A Really Hot Meal' from *The Learned Hippopotamus* by Gavin Ewart, published by Hutchinson's Children's Books. Reprinted by permission of Century Hutchinson Ltd. Eleanor Farjeon: 'Breakfast' from *Silver Sand and Snow*, published by Michael Joseph Ltd. Reprinted by permission of David Higham Associates Ltd. Max Fatchen: 'Elbows' and 'Windy' from *Wry Rhymes for Troublesome Times* by Max Fatchen, published by Kestrel Books, 1983. Copyright © Max Fatchen 1983. Reprinted by permission of Penguin Books Ltd. Roy Fuller: 'Meetings and Absences' from *Poor Roy*, by Roy Fuller. Reprinted by permission of the author. Harry Graham: 'Tender-heartedness' from *Ruthless Rhymes*. Reprinted by permission of A. P. Watt Ltd. Adrian Henri: 'Domestic Help' from *The Phantom Lollipop Lady & Other Poems*. Copyright © 1986 by Adrian Henri. Published by Methuen Children's Books. Reprinted by permission of Deborah Rogers Ltd. A. P. Herbert: 'The Spider'. Reprinted by permission of A. P. Watt Ltd. on behalf of Lady Herbert. Russell Hoban: 'Bees' from *Egg Thoughts & Other Songs*. Reprinted by permission of David Higham Associates Ltd. David Hornsby: 'Tom's Bomb' from *Allsorts 6*. Reprinted by permission of Methuen Children's Books. Laurence Houseman: 'Word of Honour' from *The New Children's Guide to Knowledge*. Reprinted by permission of Sidgwick & Jackson Ltd. Ted Hughes: 'My Other Granny' from *Meet My Folks* by Ted Hughes. Reprinted by permission of Faber & Faber Ltd. Leroy Jackson: 'Jelly Jake and Butter Bill' from *The Peter Patter Book* © 1918 Checkerboard Press, a division of Macmillan, Inc. Reprinted by permission of Macmillan Inc. X. J. Kennedy: 'The Social Mixer' from *Allsorts 7*. Reprinted by permission of Methuen Children's Books Ltd. Naomi Lewis: 'June' from *Come*

It's unbelievably simple!

Learn to draw with Rolf Harris . . .

ROLF HARRIS

YOUR CARTOON TIME

Did you know that you can draw?

Rolf Harris shows you how – clearly and simply – in YOUR CARTOON TIME. Starting with stick figures, he explains how to develop these step-by-step into your own stylish characters, and there are ideas too for how you can use your drawings – as birthday cards, home movies and so on.

Drawing is fun!

All you need is a pencil, paper and Rolf Harris's book – YOUR CARTOON TIME.

KNIGHT BOOKS

TONY ROBINSON AND RICHARD CURTIS

ODYSSEUS
THE GREATEST HERO OF THEM ALL

'They were all standing in a circle in the middle of the room; the most powerful men in the world all together. Drawing their daggers, they cut their right hands, and as the blood dripped on to the pile of gold, they swore Odysseus' vow: Helen could marry whom she liked, and the Princes would defend them both. There was a silence, broken only by the drip of red blood on gold.'

Everyone's heard of the wooden horse of Troy, haven't they? And everyone knows of the beauty of Helen – whose face once launched a thousand ships – don't they? Well this is the story the way Odysseus saw it all, from his boyhood to his participation in the bloody Trojan war itself.

Based on the exciting and award-winning BBC TV series.

KNIGHT BOOKS

TONY ROBINSON AND RICHARD CURTIS

ODYSSEUS II
THE JOURNEY THROUGH HELL

'Circe, how do we get home from here?'
asked Odysseus, putting his boots on.
Circe gently kissed his forehead and said,
'There's only one person who can tell you
that – the prophet Tyresius.'
'But he's been dead for hundreds of years!'
'Exactly,' said Circe, and unrolled a torn and
faded map. 'If you want to get home, you
must visit the Land of the Dead.'

It had taken ten long, bloody years for the
Greeks to win the Trojan War and now,
Odysseus, their victorious leader, wanted
nothing more than to return home to his
wife and son.
What he didn't know was that the journey
ahead would take more than ten years –
and the journey through Hell was only a
beginning . . .

Based on the exciting and award-winning
BBC TV series.

KNIGHT BOOKS